# A CELTIC BLESSING

*This work is dedicated to*
*Brigitte, Kathleen and Clare*

# A CELTIC BLESSING

A collection of poetry

by

## James J. Lafferty

Copyright © 2010 by James J. Lafferty

ISBN    978-0-9684991-6-0


CD Acknowledgements:
Spoken by J.J. Lafferty
Produced by James Gordon
Mastered by Karl Machat
Music performed by James Gordon
(penny whistle, bodhran, guitar, piano, percussion, accordion)
Sandra Swannell (fiddle), Christina Maree (harp), Bob Maclean
(Celtic guitar)
Pipe tunes composed and played by Iain MacKinnon of Skye
The boar image by Adam Bissonette
Recorded at McDougall Cottage, Cambridge, Ontario

Published by Paradise Books
Printed in Canada  by Thistle Printing Limited-Toronto

# *Foreword*

Recently the distinguished Nobel Laureate of Ireland, Seamus Heaney, gave a warning that modern Ireland is in danger of losing its unique spiritual values because of the onslaught of the secular economy driven by the values of the so- called "Celtic Tiger." In a lament for a lost Ireland, the Nobel Laureate characterized the Celtic Tiger as the symbol that has come to stand for modern Ireland's economic success.

The Celtic Tiger and its worshipping of the bottom line of economic globalization create a juggernaut which crushes all that resists it. Nowhere is this juggernaut more evident for modern Ireland than in the building of a motor highway directly through Tara. This is a most sacred place to the Celtic Spirit. Seamus Heaney maintains that it was Tara that gave the peoples of this land a sense of belonging to this gorgeous space in both its mythology and its history. The Celtic peoples have a long history going back as far as Galatia at the time of the emergence of the Roman Empire. For thousands of years even before the Celts, the people of this island had a distinctive cosmology, spirituality and creativity demonstrated in the art-filled mounds of the Boyne Valley. They were then, as they are now, indigenous peoples with a long history of suffering from and resisting imperial rulers.

9

Part of that indigenous struggle has been in the hosting of a deep cultural tradition that held the Celtic Spirit at the archetypal level. In this, the Celtic peoples have treasured and held a wonderful array of heroes and heroines that are second to none in their largesse. Similar to indigenous peoples of Turtle Island, the Celts have held an incredible love toward the land as sacred endowment. The loss of this deep mystique of the land is clearly evident in the desacralization of Tara. The deep story of this land and its peoples is starting to erode in modern Ireland in the wake of the Celtic Tiger.

We, Celts, desperately need modern poets and bards that will reconnect us to our magnificent cultural roots as a unique people. Seamus Heaney brings us to the wonderful riches of the tradition but we need many more poets of his kind to keep this spirit alive. James Lafferty is one such a poet. In an incredibly rich and expansive offering of blessings and poems, *A Celtic Blessing* is a treasure trove of Celtic wisdom and beauty.

In the best sense this poet is, through his work, a holder of the tradition. This deep order of identification with the ancestral peoples is felt in both word and sound in these offerings. He is a poet living in the diaspora of Canada and holding a longing for his native land. This anthology, in both word and sound, starts with a blessing, through which he invokes the primordial powers to gift his readers with the poetic offerings to follow. Because of the history of suffering of the Irish at the hands of imperial conquerors, many of the poems are lamentations on exile, wandering and pilgrimage.

Nevertheless we are invited by this poet to a deep affirmation of life and land.

The sense of the Earth as nurturing mother is made palpable in many of these offerings. There is a haunting echo of the transcendent in the midst of luxurious earthiness. James Lafferty's poetry does not dwell in past history. He connects his poetic utterances with the larger global world in which we live. His closing blessing on the four directions connects Celtic wisdom with the profound wisdom of First Nations Peoples living on Turtle Island. It is a calling forth of the indigenous peoples of every land.

This collection of poetry is accompanied with a CD disc ("A Celtic Blessing") that contains the poems of the book's first section in sound and dramatically rendered in voice by James Lafferty. The background music hosts the readings. Once heard in this manner you are made aware of the power of poetic utterance as part of the oral tradition. The poet's gift of language organizes sound, sense and intuition into a perfect whole.

**Edmund O'Sullivan**
December 2009

# TABLE OF CONTENTS

13

**Part Two: A Selection from the CD: Seeking the Stones**

## Part One: A CELTIC BLESSING

## I Prelude

## A CELTIC BLESSING

Bless to you the way under your feet.

Bless to you the hope in your swelling hearts.

Bless to you the love spilling from your soul-charged

eyes.

May you be able to hear each other in the soft rustle of

your fears.

May you be balm to each other's brokenness.

May you be to each other in anxious moments the

tree's shade in the heat of the day.

May you be a fruitful branch on the tree of life –

burgeoning with vitality and bountiful grace.

May the branches of your being
bridge the gap between you -
but may you not lean too heavily
on each other - bending your true shape.

May your joys be as plentiful as the grass and sorrows
drop sparsely  to flow swiftly away.
May you have courage to dare and wisdom to seize
your chances which fade like the colours of Spring.
In the hushed stillness of your souls, may you build
your place of peace.

May you be full in your living.
May you be deep in your thinking.
May you be endless in your loving.
And may the Creator - God keep you in the eye of his
compassion  forever.

## II Origins

### "Mystery"

In the solstice of the thin time

the shadow falls

between birth and life

held in balance –

the time of no time –

when light lies lambent

in the cries

of a baby born dying

caught in the hinge

between the formless and form,

between the advent and the leaving,

between the leap of light

and the density of the dark,

between the breath and the hesitation,

between the shortest day

and the turn of the sun,

between the beat and its missing,

between the past and what's to come.


This time, when mystery

haunts the breath of day

and death is banished once more

as the cycle spirals out,

climbing with the newborn son.


In the moment, time pauses.

In the newness of his days,

he holds the light

and the dark

within him.

Born in the thin time

of the sacred cycle,

he struggles for life,

unravelling the knotted folds of death,

leaping at last into

the lap and lustre of life.

.

## "Enlightened"

The leerie, like a squire of light,

moved smartly from one lamppost

to the next

as he bore his wand through the gathering mist;

desirous, no doubt, to be home

relishing his favourite dish.


The job, a chore to him,

was mystery, magic, wonder

to the little one who followed

and watched him –

a lilting Lugh in the gloaming

light up the night.

**"Elemental"**

He was like a 'weeble" – a wobbly man,

my father – no matter what

hit him he bounced back.


He did amazing things:

like pick up burning coal

with his bare hands;

flip himself over

from an essentially

standing position –

he once flipped himself

from the window ledge

of our upper storey flat

and landed,

cat-like, on his feet.


While he belonged to the earth

in a very elemental way,

even when he was

another kind of wobbly man-

he often carried stars in his pocket.

## The Pictures

Those great moon nights

when the ground rivalled

the stars for glitter,

somnambulist,

hooked on my mother's arm,

leaning in to her warmth,

home up the hill

in the sharp, crisp air.


Running images

of the film just seen:

bereft orphans,

a p.o.w. escaping the stalag,

a sheep farmer facing tremendous odds

up against the ruthless cattle barons,

the natives' trail of tears —

I was the hero

of these night journeys —

these dreams on the fly.


Wishing the yards ahead

were yards behind.

Home to tea and toast,

then to a water-bottled warmed bed —

the smell of fire passing

through the house

from living to bedroom.


I remember, Irene,

those romantic, heroic episodes

in The Hall and The Strand —

Mario Lanza, Randolph Scott,

Gene Kelly, Audie Murphy,

Doris Day, Debbie Reynolds

and all the rest

marching, riding, dancing, singing

through my mind.


The pictures with my mother -

little flickers of paradise -

treats thrown my way

as the youngest of the brood.



These memories glow,

like the silver shadows,

with warmth and love;

soft images against

the harsh screen of reality

held over for life.

## "Light in the Darkness"

The flakes – soft and self-absorbed – fell silently. He brushed them off with his left hand as the right buried itself deep in his coat pocket. He was in a rush with only ten minutes before Mass started. Midnight Mass, Christmas Midnight Mass. Without money for the local all-night dance, not even money to buy a packet of cigarettes, he had decided to forego morning Mass and a warm bed to go to the romantically-hued Midnight Mass. This Mass gave the sense of the primary occasion – light entering the darkness, warmth in the cold, hope born into despair.

Life seemed at a low ebb that year – not unusual for that time and place. He worked in a market garden – low wage an eighth of it gone on bus fares alone- not much left for frills. Living at home, he felt like a mill-stone weight pulling his parents down. Christmas increased the pressure though his people never flinched – while they had little, they cared much.

He hurried on assured and expectant of the church's warmth. He entered quickly, dipped a hand in the font. Its water warm in comparison. He found a place to the right and knelt. The organ leapt to life with a "Hark the Herald Angels" and the Mass was underway. Singing lustily, he meditated on the message of peace that the night proclaimed and his heart lifted. Mass over, he left quickly and walked hurriedly home. It was painfully apparent that he had no smokes and it left him on edge. He had badgered his mother for a cigarette earlier and she had "lent him one." This had been hours ago. After a brisk walk, he reached his door. Going in, he moved directly into the kitchen to put the water on for tea. Turning into the living room, he saw there on the table a small glass of sherry, three Swan Vestas matches and two cigarettes, Santa had come early and again his heart lifted.

## III History

## "Anglesey 61 A.D."

Fierce moans from Mona, insula sacra,

assail our ears,

Druids, their sacred priests,

holders of their hearts,

line the shore,

hoping to distract, dispirit us

with their vibrant, magical curses.

Their womenfolk, arrayed in black,

bearing firebrands,

their hair snaking the wind,

howl like lost souls

in the hold of Hades.

The damning cries rend

the grizzled dawn.


Ice pellets from the North bite our faces.

We land and, though fearful,

set to our task

with learned,  practiced efficiency.

The Druids and their baying Furies,

we slaughter

and leave their holy groves scorched;

laying to rest

a threat to Roman peace.


The severed head of this race,

the core of their faith,

lies on the reddened sand of Mona.

And we in this far northern cold

dream of the warmth of Terracina

far, far away from this alien,

feral and phantom-filled land.

.

## "To Hell or Connaught"

> "Here I am my back to the wall,
>
> playing tunes unto empty pockets" O'Raftery

To feel bereft of sustenance

at the end of your day

the best gone from you

no hearth your own.

With patron, dead or fled,

you stitch a rhyme together

holding strands of bygone days

in your shaken spirit.

To be without succour

in the absence of light,

nothing to nourish you

in the oncoming night.

Your cry cuts across the years

to penetrate the heart.

O irreparable loss, desolate bard,

displaced, morose and impoverished.


Pain that permeates to the bone

and cracks the soul is the mantle you bear.


Rough fields and poor soil

were the remnant left to the Gael,

dispossessed and pushed to the margins.

Strangers in their own land,

they are no longer sheltered under

the chieftain's largesse.

The clan system shattered,

leaving shards and fragments

of a former world fading

as they watched.

The chieftains have fled

from loss and pain,

the people remain

in their sorrow,

lamenting dispersal and displacement,

dispossessed, at one stroke,

of their leaders and their lands.


Removed from the hearth

that heated and held the heart.

Sat down by the highway,

with the threads of my life

frayed and fluttering

in the storm of my rage

Paupers now, we once were

kin to kings.

Our ways overwhelmed by

a deluge of strangers.


From an oasis to a desert,

from paradise to Hades

without a Lethe to wash away

the nettle of memory.

We move, as though dead,

westward, in the cold grey of November

hassled  and harassed by the soldiery,

who benefit from our misery,

granted our horses and our holdings

as pay.


A stained and rocky trail of tears.

From largesse to leanness,

from plenty to penury,

from brightness to bleakness,

from nurturing hearth to desolate heath.

The smoored ashes of the clans,

the embers of our tradition,

are scattered in the Puritan wind

of a calloused army,

the driving sword of change

held by a zealot,

who saw the "mere" Irish

as uncivilized, less than human.


Wave upon wave hit the rugged coast,

later to embark across the sea,

landless, broken and uprooted –

chaff on the wind of fate.

Postscript:


The generous lords are gone,

the praise of the chieftains silenced.

Only a curse left on the lips of the bard:

"May the maggots in the void of Hell

gnaw at your heart, Cromwell, for ever.


And may the High King of Heaven bring again

our valleys and fields to our keeping."

Note:
This Irish trail of tears foreshadows the many walked by the clans of
Turtle Island..

## "Las Cinco Heridas"


Poverty is my oppressive crown,

thorns wound in terror.

My right hand riven

with the pain of ignorance.

My left hand lashed

by fear.

My feet fastened

with nails of famine.

In my side

I feel despair – as my blood drips

on this land stigmatized.

Eloi, Eloi, lama sabachtani?

Why have you forsaken me?

I am El Salvador – The Saviour.

Ecce homo de los pobres.

Who will be Christ enough

to uncrucify me?

## "Las Flores de la Calle"

In the shadow of the cathedral,
they die.
Their crime is breathing
the same air as the tourists
who flock to see the gilded beauties
of the city.

In the shadow of the cathedral,
they lived
huddled together for warmth,
to feel they belonged,
a family of vulnerabilities
linked for strength

against the pain within,

and the indifferent city without.


In the shadows of the cathedral,

the guns fire.

The children are baptized

with their blood,

their brief lives flowing away.


Flores de la calle

laid like an offering

by the cathedral's walls,

their breathing stopped,

where the money shifts hands

and the Te Deum fills the air

in the dark shadow

of the cold stone.

**"A Cleansing of the Soul"**

Shut beauty up
with the ravished and the simple,
with those who need love
and in their longing err.

Ravishing beauty entices the young
and better it wasn't there
better hidden,
encased in ugliness.

The simple can be led to bed
or anywhere.

They thus have need of firm guidance,

and where better to receive such aid

than from holy, mother church,

where passion is tamed.

Young love-seekers,

pleading for acceptance

bear children as children,

but must not be permitted

to bring blame to their parents

and shame to their church

by allowing bastards

(ostracized by the world)

to be flaunted.


Christ's wounds!  That would be madness.

Better by far to enslave

those wayward souls,

have them repent in

the steam and sweat of a laundry.

Whilst cleaning themselves up for Our Lord,

they earn money for us poor sisters.

Their seeming chains are gleaming,

their cleansing a boon of bountiful grace.

Everybody wins.


Through the damp darkness of their drudgery,

strumpets of sin, harlots of heaven,

we save their souls, Persil white,

for God.

.

# IV The Journey

## "The Journey"

*For Kate of Fallowfield, Manchester*

The poem was written twenty years after the note was presented on a grey Manchester evening to him as a young, unsure man about to return to Glasgow on the overnight bus.

The story began a few years previously. At sixteen, he had gone south to Manchester to find work. He rode down on the back of his brother's Matchless 500 – swaying on the pillion down the blustery Pennines. He moved away from his brother not long thereafter, having found employment at the CWS, 1 Balloon St., Manchester as an Accounts Clerk in the H Department and digs with a Catholic family from South Shields. It was in the CWS employ that he was to meet Kate from M Department. She and her friend would pass him each day at lunch as he took up his station outside the Bank building which housed their departments. He would stand in the shaft of sunlight which fell between the huddled buildings, having a smoke and longing for home.

"What's your name?"

"Joe."

"My friend, Kate, fancies you and wonders if you would be willing to go out with her some time?"


Kate and he dated for a fair length of time. In fact, for the rest of his stay in the city, over three years all told. They became deeply involved, so much so that he began to wonder about the idea of a mixed marriage. He, at that age, was not prepared to wrestle with the identity life had fashioned. His life was like a tapestry which had as its most significant weaves his Irish-Catholic faith. To pull on these particular threads was to unravel the whole. An Irish Catholic from the West of Scotland working class was part of a meshed fabric in terms of religion, politics, and the Glasgow team he favoured. Pull at the bulk of these threads and the piece became tatters or that was what he thought. The idea of marrying someone from across the dyke was hard to sustain. He sought to avoid it and one way of doing so was to cut and run, to return north. His homesickness was acute anyway.

He had doubts about his general feelings about Kate She was a very sweet and loving girl. Yet he was unsure of committing so early, unsure of what it would mean with regard to the looming Mother Church – a shadow of doubt and guilt. When he told the sorrowful Kate of his decision to return home, she was deeply sad and he felt bad that he was the root of her dismay.

So painful was the tear in their lives that he asked her not to come to the bus depot the night that he was leaving. The bus was due to leave around 10:00 p.m. to arrive in Glasgow about 5:30 a.m.. He told her that it was unnecessary to come to see him off, but she ignored him. She came, her grey eyes welling with the overflow of her great heart. She gave him a note in a pink envelope and told him not to open it until the bus was underway.

When he read the note somewhere outside the city limits, he wanted to turn the bus around to return to the source of such sentiment. He felt filled with sorrow – a sense of grievous loss. The potent note expressed a love that he had never imagined, that had been beyond his ken before this. He was nonplussed and lost.

Later his mother, who had met Kate on a visit to Manchester, was to tell him that she cried when she thought of his leaving Kate. This was highly ironic as it was his mother who had been the most influential on shaping his faith which was one of the major barriers against the relationship. How human and humane, however, for his mother to feel Kate's pain like that – another model that perhaps he should have followed.

He did not see her again after that night in the bus station, in the Manchester rain, but twenty years later she came into his heart with such force that he penned "The Journey." He had only one desire that the poem reach Kate's hand and that she gain back what she gave so compellingly so long ago.

## "The Journey"

Overcast

Manchester skies,

grey steel,

your grey eyes –

pleading.

It had rained

all day

and as it ends,

so runs our round.


In the concrete coldness,

you press into my hand

a blood-warmed note:

pink envelope against

the white –

a crushed carnation

of your love.


I have no words.

Though my heart returns

as I read –

the bus heads on  -

nosing the North -

while the ice of me

melts in the warmth of you.


I have it still – and when-

unloved or unloving –

I take it out

to touch such love again:

I hold a compass for the heart.

## "The Weft"


When we touch earth,

we touch all the earth.

So I am with you,

even when I am away.

The breath that is the wind

blows freely over

the face of the earth

and as my breath

mingles with it,

so too does it mingle

with your breath

and we are one.

A shaman once told me

that when I sing aloud

in the outdoors here

that I make connection

as a keeper

with Dunadd.

Though I am here

the sound will be present there

reverberating, resounding

in the heart of the stone.

## "The Echo of the Maya"

The voice of the Maya,
like a river-vein coursing
the earth,
flows to bring life
to the hearers —
an all-encompassing prayer
of the four directions.

I hear the voices
of the disappeared
echoing, reverberating
in the defiant words
of an aggrieved Guatemalan grandmother

standing outside the Fort Benning fence

behind which  Latino military

are taught to use the tools of terror,

the implements of pain.


Her courage is a flame

flaring in a benighted world.

Falling over the nefarious place,

her steady voice,

soft and  strong,

unshaken and unshakeable,

squeezes  the heart.


Her sons tortured in

the horror of a Guatemalan night

by the mechanical, inhuman force

trained mere steps away

beyond the razor wire.

In a place where human dignity is defiled.

In a place where the worst elements in man are honed.

In a place where light fails to penetrate.

In a place diseased and contaminating.

In a place of the jackal and the carrion crow.


Your face, Julio, hermano, is unrecognizable,

they have numbered all your bones,

they have castrated all your dreams,

gouged out  your soul

and left the shell of you

on a festering dump.


Your spirit yet haunts the highlanda

and breathes on the Pacific shore

in the hearths and in the hearts

of your people. !Presente!

Your voice echoes in the waves

and through the coconut leaves,

stirring the constancies of the land.

## "Epiphany"

A babe presented –
made manifest –
in the early morning
of a cold winter's day.

A young woman,
full blown in maternal glory,
radiant and proud
over what she had made,
gave to me
wrapped in her buoyant joy
a gift – an epiphany –

shining through the cold and dark

the surge to life,

a persistence of the human soul.


There before me a little person

held up from behind

by her sustaining mother,

a splendour of the spirit

shining forth in the midst

of dark times

beckoning to life

and a woman

telling me

of the treasure

hidden in the mantle

of her motherhood.

I felt the Goddess move

in the energy of her soul,

the rising of the green-fused tree,

lightning leapt from sky to earth,

the water welled,

the air shivered

and the promise of ages

smiled

blessing our frozen ground.

.

## "The Eternal Moment"

*"Partake of the sacrament of every living moment."*

*R.D.Laing*

Hail, holy life –

free- flowing soul

caught, encased

yet aware

conscious of

the eternal in

drops of water,

grains of trees.

Holy, holy, hold for
our heart, smothered
sometimes so we miss
the beat eternal
never feel the harp play,
taste the wind,
see the vital flower.

Holy, unwhole,
unholy,
we hide from vitality
seek shelter
from our weakness,
find holes in which to hide,
until the fetid air
blinds us
and we drown in darkness.

Let light break in

to the damp soul.

Hail, holy light.


Let us perceive

the sacredness of life,

in here and in now.

Hail and climb

with each pulsing moment.


Let us partake

in the bright of

new-found day,

see haloes on the hillside,

saintliness in a stranger's eyes,

taste with tongues afire

the living stream of

all our days.

.

## " Experience"

Where are the whispers

that stir the soul to

reach beyond?

In the still echo

of the heart hides

the truth so hard to face.


To be content is elusive

when the butterfly of promise

flutters near the net

of your desire -

the beginning of suffering.

.

## "The Sparrow"

Blank of snow

drapes the dormant mother,

still the sleeping seed waits

to rise.

This is all there is,

this is our story,

birth, death and rising

arrayed in muted glory.

The cycle moves,

the circle completes,

and we search

the mystery for meaning

we can glean

of birth, life and death.


The tale of the sparrow,

Eadwine's admonishment,

a bird flying through the great hall

from immensity to immensity,

from dark to dark,

with but a moment

hanging in between.

## "A Still Moment at Rattlesnake Point"

A thought of transience,

a fallen leaf,

in the late summer

of my life.

My two daughters

ahead of me,

as we walk in

the stillness.

This day

will never happen again.

A bright moment

amidst the shadow,

Kathleen and Clare,

framed by trees,

snapped and placed

firmly in my memory.

Their images always set

in my soul –

their laughter echoes

in the chambers of my heart.

I hurry after them

through the light-bright woods.

This day

will never happen again,

but I will always be

looking after them –

caught

in this passing moment.

## "The Coat"

*"The road is laid out," she said,*

*"and you will cover the needed ground*

*to reach the throne of heaven."*

I carry my motley threads of life

and will eventually wear a coat

of their weave.

We gather the threads

from tests and trials,

from the spoils and spills,

the gifts and gladness

of our unfolding, enfolding life.


The spun threads from the wheel

are formed and worked

with the dye of time

and the shuttle of circumstance,

woven by the woof of the heart

and the weft of the soul

into a beaded raiment

that shimmers and casts light

for the watchful, discerning eye.

# V The Celtic Core

## "Makin'"

I would draw silence o'er me like a cloak,

ruminate in the dark heat of my heart -

the bellows worked with

the rhythmic breath of the soul.

Shape my words into the echo

of my soul's pleading

which rests far  beyond words,

beyond all the smoke, mirrors and

pretences of the world.

I would draw silence o'er me like a cloak,

search in the pool of my being

for its verities,

stones of truth waiting to be found,

for plucking, polishing and preserving

in a form

poignant, graceful.and compelling.


I would draw silence o'er me like a cloak,

blot out the vagaries of

the workaday, "I'm okay" world,

seek the centre

and plumb the soul's depth,

touch the pulse that beats

in time with the source.


I would draw silence o'er me like a cloak,

listen to the pulse

feel its steadiness, and

hear its quiet murmur,

search the space within

and carry the core,

beating to the surface.


I would draw silence o'er me like a cloak,

to sing the song of my soul,

where it sits in the stillness –

a lotus- blossom

on the pool of eternity-

moving to the music

of the Oran  Mor.


I would draw silence o'er me

like a great cloak

of darkness,

to compose with

the rough stone

on my flesh

prodding wakefulness

and awareness of the soul

clapping to its rhythm

-forging words on

the face of eternity.

## The Beare Peninsula


I, a returning child, sit

in the embrace of my mother,

my queen, my goddess.


I am realized here,

as Ferdia.

What was glimpsed, becomes apparent.


Exile, wanderer, seeker,

I open the hasp of my soul

and let the light of your power

fall upon the fields of my being.

Fecund one, enfold me.

Let the salve of your healing

revivify and enlighten,

let it quell doubts

and leave my soul laughing

enjoined in the dance of life.

## "Callanish"

*We bend to blow it now to flame*

*to pass it on. ("Ours Has Been Exile")*


Callanish, Tursachan,

place of pilgrimage

on the far margins

of the world,

where the stones stand

holding history and mystery.

Miles from the mainland

a sanctuary – the sacred

held in stone

lasting, weather-lashed

latent power

lambent on its forms.

Light and bright the day

on which we come

bearing in our hearts

the quest for the sacred,

seeking intimations

of the eternal

in the stones.


In the still silence

close to the cairn,

we stand filming

and taking still shots

of the sleeping stones,

static and steady

in the summer sun.

We are alone

enwrapped in our single devotion,

until she comes

like a vision, a muse,

an aisling, a manifestation

of the sacred –

a goddess in blue jeans.


Bearing a flute,

she takes her place

in the centre –

the cairn-

place of ancient bones.

She plays

sitting at the heart

of the stones.

She offers her blessing

in the holy space,

feeding in an act of reciprocity

the mother of the moors -

the sustainer.

Acolyte, priestess,

she sanctifies the place

with her thurible of sound.


She is a keeper,

a holder of the tradition,

a pilgrim through time,

who captures the numen

in her presence, in her act.

Tursachan – the place of pilgrimage

is again affirmed,

as she moves off

as softly and swiftly as she came

out of the site –

away – over the hill

and out of sight.


As the keeper disappears,

the tourists come

for their ten minutes of gawking,

until they move on to the wee shop

for their tea and T shirts.

In us, the flame is kindled-

ours to feel its sacred warmth,

to nourish it, to keep it,

and find the words and ways

to pass it on.


A sacred fire on a summer's day

from away, far away,

in the place of pilgrimage - Tursachan –

the site of the sacred stones.

## "Endurance"

Like pollinating bees,

a myriad of flowers,

spilling rainbows on the ancient steps,

the women of the Maya

as colourfully dressed

as their wares.


Above the river of vibrant hues,

the grey steps rise

carrying the men upwards

their perforated cans  wafting

incense into the bright

Guatemalan air,

as old women

kneel on the gnarled stone,

atoning.


At the top,

rising from the ruins

of a Mayan temple,

the white stucco

of Santo Tomas,

where the people weave their primal

with the alien faith of the conquistadores.

The stairs on which they move,

they moved on,

standing or kneeling,

in the far distant past.

Their souls still rooted,

their spirit unbowed.


In Ireland, many pilgrims

swarm up Croagh Patrick

penitential feet bare,

to climb three hours

as the saint himself did.

And where the druids,

long before Patrick

saw the sun,

stood to honour Lug

on this timeless and

eternally sacred space.

.

## "Water"

Mother – river, sustainer,

Bearer of gifts,

Earth embracer,

pour forth in your might.

Hold us, carry us

on our vital journey,

do not cast us off early

or hold us too long.

Within your graces bless us.

In the depth

of your grandness and power

bear us

and when the frail raft

of our going

finds its end,

wash over us gently

and flow on.

## "Translation"

The rhythm of the primal sea

beats ceaselessly on Connemara stone.

The place in Gaelic, Cloch na Ron

(stone of the seals)

anglicized – Roundstone

the mystery evaporates.

Stone of the seals- a touchstone

for shared community.

The play of seals

on a sun-drenched rock

The sigh of the seal-

a human mime

through the mist,

a cry in the briny air,

like a mother keening a lost child.


The evocative eyes,

liquid and lamenting,

sealing  a pact with fellow mortals.

In those depths, hints

of a consolation

and commonality

translated  by the swimmers of the stone

into the human heart.


Perhaps, they are

human souls -

revisiting stone -

lost at sea.

## "A Tremor of the Heart"

Bless to your ears the crashing waves.

Bless to your eye the whale spouting

in the deep channel.

Bless to your heart the majestic ice-mountains flowing

by.

Bless to you your foot-tread on sand and stone.

The earth, your mother, welcomes you,

be ever respectful of her sustenance.


Bless to you the breath that is the wind.

Bless to you the light and warmth of Brother Sun.

Bless to you the rising of the moon.

Bless to your tongues the life-bearing rain.

Bless to you the perfection that is the tree.

Bless to you the singing of the waterfall.

Bless to you the luminaries of the night.

Bless to you the confluence of the waters.

Bless to you the light and bright of flower and snow-
flake.


Bless to you the company of the four-leggeds, the
swimming tribe
and the clan of choristers in the air.


Bless to you the shining path.

Bless to you the moments of sadness,

may they deepen you and help you grow –

but never, never stop your flow.

May you flourish with ability to discern

and the true warmth of a compassionate heart.

Bless to you the bond of two:

when one walks in the dark,

the other will bring light;

when one feels pain,

the other will bear liniment;

when one weeps,

the other will feel a tremor in the heart.

.

## The Sustainer


I am the rainfall that sustains the earth.

I am the sun's blessing on the bending wheat.

I am the wind-carried seed.

I am the harvest that enlivens the throng.

I am the windfall from the blessing tree.

I am the teeming udder of the belling cow.

I am the full blossoms on a summer's day.

I am the fruit of all that bears.

I am the bee-borne pollen.

I am the gold of the hive.

I am the horn of plenty.

I am the height of summer.

I am the waxing of the sea.

I am the growing in the children.

I am the burgeoning of talent.

I am optimism in the eyes of youth.

I am the laughter in the soul.

I am the contentment of the giver.

I am the blessing for those who receive.

I am the weaver of dreams.

I am the shaper of fate.

I am the tree of life.

I am the break in the fall.

I am the dawn in your darkness.

I am the sustainer of all.

## "A Celtic Prayer of the Four Directions"

"Poetry flows through me – ice from the North"

May the Lord of the Elements

bring the brightness of Lugh, the long-armed,

casting the first light of day-

place of life's beginning,

initiator of young dreams,

walking illuminated over the earth

dawn, wafted on the eagle's wings

bringing sight and insight

heralding the surge – sap of Spring,

the pulse

coursing and pushing

against the mantle of the dark

the frigid ground, the hoar frost

of the sleeping mother,

the clarion call of clarity,

the gradual liberation of

the benighted earth.


Bless the people of the East

may they walk warmly

in the sun that is always rising.


Creator, bless the South

and all who dwell there

in the place of fire

and abundant life, where

the howl of the coyote permeates

and the song of life

plays full and strong.

Life resplendent-

fecund and feral.

The place of the overflowing heart

the burgeoning of life

the fire in the belly

the green fuse driving with

elemental force.


The place of the sustainer –

Brigid, the exalted one,

daughter of Dagda,

who gives of herself

so that her children

may thrive.


Bless the people of the South,

may their dance always

embrace the deepest rhythms of life.

May the Great Spirit move

over the peoples of the West,

the direction of descent

of the sun and of life.


The lair of the bear,

the place of completion

and satisfaction.


The realm of the Cailleach,

her change and memory.

The place of the hearth's fire,

the remnant of the day,

a place of introspection

searching, reviewing

the path of life-

seeing through the coming night,

which opens for us all,

to the fruits of the spiritual harvest.

Bless the process of autumn –

the glory of colour

and the annual death – bearing seeds

of resurrection.

Bless the people of the West,

the keepers of the medicine

of the soul,

the elixir of Manitou.

Bless to us the land of the polar bear

and the snow goose,

the place of the intelligence

and the cold, dark winter

Night – where the body is restored

and the land sleeps

held  in snow and ice –

fallow,  but not forlorn

still,  though not desolate.


May the frozen tundra be hallowed

the caribou on their endless treks,

the snowy owl, the seal,

the migrating Canada geese.

May the snow be blessed.

May the skidoo never fail.

May the Cailleach Bheur

continue to evolve

from her harsh hue

to her lustrous aspect

that adorns her resurrection

in the vernal Spring.

May the cold never  penetrate

the people of the midnight sun.

May the light within burn brightly

in the endless dark mystery

that is North.


May the peoples of the Four Directions

walk life's path with care and in peace,

aware of their bonds, one with the other,

and the common urge to live

we bear as human beings

on this small planet, known as Earth.

Slainte agus beannachtai

.

## Part Two: A selection from the CD:

## Seeking the Stones

**"A Hymn for Clare Aisling"**

I   A light fed
        in the dark
                breaks.

   In a wave of flame,
   your light finds light.

   Your mother throbbed
   her life to you –
   a living coil.

You suck air –

you flash your eyes

blink, wink at the world.


Your skin furred, your hair wet,

 cave-dark.

You rage against the passing warm,

'til tired and tried

you sleep.


II  A pulsing line

   to your mother's land

   brings cries, as though

   the Earth Mother sings:

   Freude, Freude, Freude!

   Triumphant joy enwraps you,

   may your life unravel so,

   meine kleine Tochter.

III  Hope from the dark,

grace us.

Beam of heaven,

bless us.

Bead of night,

guide us.

Beat of the earth,

embrace us.

In sorrow, you console us.

In joy, you join us.

Abundance of life,

enthrall us.

I bend over your beauty,

my sad joy mingles with your cries

bonded together.


IV  Herald of joy,

may you help

re-store our vision,

re-cover our bright dream,

re-form our fractured light,

and re-member our broken

unity

## "Brokenness"

We are shards

of our shattered dreams

jagged, wounding and wounded

in our incompleteness.

We move, drifting together,

to make a new form,

but fail to fit exactly;

there are holes

where the dark seeps through

destroying the dotted lines

to any destination.

The dark is empty

save for the whimper

and the whisper of a last song,

a light laughter and

brighter days that like butterflies pass

fleetingly away,

through holes

where the light never comes

and the dotted lines

of destination are invisible.

## "The Old Man"

The old man stands,

tears running down his gullied

cheeks.

Old man, why are you weeping?

Is it because babies are born

without teeth

and only pain will bring them

through the gum?

Is it because this child is blind

and that lame

and life's demands leave them

wavering in the dark?


Is it because a young mother grew

old in giving birth to a son

without fingers?


Is it because the deserts of Arabia

are skeleton-strewn,

or that the Wailing Wall

sheds tears?


Is it because the fields of

Cambodia smell of blood,

or that with fiery tar Ireland

brands those who fraternize?

Is it because the river which

ran, now limps with debris,

or that the woodland has

faded and fallen before

speculative greed?


Is it because we could all

vanish in a cloud of a

technical error?



Is it because you are grey,

and your sap is drying,

and you feel

death's frigid fingers

searching your sparse hair?

Is it because your nest

is bare

and loneliness sits

by your fire?

Old man, why are you weeping?

## "The Clyde"

Artery of our being

named for the goddess –

giver and sustainer.

Today,

they bring strange gifts:

a rusting shopping cart

thrust into your waters

and a drum,

circle of steel,

corroding near your bank –

sad votives

in a spiritless time.

.

## "Dunadd"

As I stood on rock
where the kings of Dalriada
stood,
Christian was not how I felt.

The wind, eerie and singular,
reinforced the sense of mystery,
the sacred, that dwelt there
in the shifting light.

Totemic boar etched in rock:
a bridge to the Otherworld,
spiritual guide and nourishment.

His fierce, wild , untamed essence

drawn on to imbue mettle

in those he faced.

Here, the newly crowned

took on his tenacity and courage.


A place too for regal foot

where the king vowed

to continue the culture of his people

and hold sacred the gods

our people swore by,

until Dalriada, like Tara, passed

and the grieving wind now blows

the grass around the hill of Dunadd.


Ogham – language of mystery,

script of trees,

lines of the druid,

the dance of meaning

in a meaningful place.

The centre now shaped

to the margins,

as the world moves

and the new wind weaves

the grasses and kisses the script

incised on the crowning rock

of a faded kingdom.


On this height, I was

connected –

as stone, plain, stream,

and keening wind

conjured a moment of grace,

a gift of continuity to me.

By the gods my people swear by,

I pledge the same.

.

## " The Passage Grave"

The swirl of the cycle holds

within its wheel

the rhythm of life.

We build our graves

and bury our dead

in stones

fashioned to last

and shaped to hold

our hope of rebirth.

On the shortest day

of the turning world,

when the sun hides his face

for the longest time,

his rays penetrate

the hidden depth of Earth

and as the Mother opens herself

to the golden flood,

we live.


Mother of the dark,

mystery and germ,

Holder of life,

Keeper of the heart,

open yourself

to the cascading light.

The cold recedes,

the waters flow again.

## "The Chieftain"

You have gone from us now.

You who strongly stood

against all our foes.

Your stout heart steadfast

in hours of great trial.

In times of peace,

the glint of your happy eye

fell upon all who came before you –

blessing them.


Your wit radiant

in your cordial repast,

where your generosity showed

135

in the welcome of all to your board.

You touched their very soul,

 Chieftain, o my cherished chieftain!

Now the keen of the women

rises and rips the mist

of this sorrowful morning.

You have gone from us.


It seems only yesterday

you rode to Tara,

radiant and powerful

in your full regalia.

A silver boar pendant

glinting in the early light-

Man amongst men.

Prince of princes,

Warrior of warriors –

your prowess was perennial,

your table was renowned,

your judgment honoured,

your honesty a guiding light.

Chieftain among men,

valiant and resolute,

gentle to the innocent,

just to the guilty,

delight to children,

dread of the knave.

You have gone from us now.


Lion of the pride,

keen of eye, wealth of wit,

counsellor of the bereft,

comforter in our woe,

shield in the storms,

light in the shadows,

shelter of the downtrodden,

keeper of the trove,

holder of the traditions,

protector against the onslaught,

earthly arm of the angels,

gone from us.


Gone is the heartful man.

Gone are the generous meals.

Gone the laughter in the hall,

gone the warmth in the dun.

Scattered are the kinsmen,

now the core has gone.

Our hearts swim in sorrow.

Landless, lord less we roam –

anchorless in a sea of loss and lamenting.


Chieftain, o my chieftain,

yeast to the heart's dough,

lord of the welcomes,

your board was hospitable,

your humanity a burning flame

in the frost of the wide world.

You have gone from us.


We stand on stony ground

grieving your passing.

The bard is left without song,

save the keen's sharp edge

rising from a sundered heart.


Ice has come early to the land.

Snow enwraps the glens

and shrouds the graves

of our fathers.

No more shall I tongue praise

of the chieftain, as my fathers did

for his fathers for generations,

for the gander has flown

to other climes.


Now I am left

by the sty wall

singing laments

in a world forlorn –

for you have gone from us.

**"Stones"**

The hearthstone is cold
  as the walls are tumbled,
the millstone of commerce
rests on the backs of the evicted
as they stagger distraught
past the milestone
of their ruined homestead.

They have nowhere to go
cast out into
the shivering eve –

a landlord with a heart of stone

measures

his property improved

without their poverty –

they are left

to wander the road

(where the stones are

not bread)

but cut

their ill-shod feet.


The menacing air

rattles their skeletal frames

and the moon is still

to rise.

## "Exile"

Like roughcast tombstones, the ruins

remembering community,

stand bearing witness –

dead the hearth's fire,

dead the lilting song,

dead the laughter

and tears have turned

to stone.


McCrae, McGinnis, MacDonald

driven, like cattle,

to the shore-

boarding the creaking ships,

with quaking heart,

lamenting ruefully in

the bleating air.


With keening souls,

they pass over

the vast, seething Atlantic –

a grave of dreams –

with memories and loss

in their heaving hearts,

they taste the salt

of their days.


In Cape Breton, their hands,

do unfamiliar work.

And their Gaelic tongue is proscribed

as a language for peasants

not people.


Shades of Culloden's defeat

hover over these hills

that mirror their own.

Once more they are at the edge,

once more they live on an island,

close to the sea

and close to the margin.

Uneasy in the land of trees,

they wrap the familiar around them

naming their new places

to reverberate the old –

Iona, Inverness, Loch Lomond –

Gaels at the edge of the world.

One hundred and fifty years later,

I, reared by the Bonnie Banks, stand

like a child of Lir metamorphosed,

in the Shamrock Club of Dominion,

feeling, for the first time

since I arrived in Toronto

twelve years earlier,

at home –

warm in the ice of Canada.

## "Felix Culpa"

I

"O essence of joy, sensual pleasures core,

my eyes are blighted

by the wonders of your flesh;

I soar, stagger and fall –

drunken with your all.

Tonight, my thrush, is dunkeld black.

My heart heaves in desperate cries –

to cover my wounds

with the lineament of lust:

tourniquet against the blood-flood

that breaks the dam of my soul.

Ah, to nuzzle my fears

upon the softness of your breast

and float my anguish

on the lusty camel's back –

my seed spraying forth

relieving this shivering vessel.


Oh, that I might forgo this cup

and let this night pass from me.

Black night when truth is crucified

and the demonic world rejoices.

See! Atlas shrugs of his burden

and Lucifer's star

creeps toward the sun.

I have below this tattered robe,

a rose plucked from that garden,

as red as the blood that spurts

from his bleeding, beaten head

and in this purse, bright silver

a gleam for a king –

ah! let's to the nearest inn

that I might drown this agony in a wine vat –

dance and sing - then, darling,

we shall to bed

to love until the dawn.

Here, I place this rose

within the lustre of your hair."


II


"Did you hear that?

Nail –driven hands!

The anvils are clanging in Hell.

Your golden hair darkens –

the rose thorns

and what you grow a beard?


Hell's curse, woman,

do you mock me?

Your hands bleed,

water pours from your side.

What iced claw clasps my heart?

Let me in!

And frenzied let me be relieved!

What impotent -

powerless  to know you?


Do not touch me!

Nay - - my mind's diseased

and it's spreading - -

I see the ants shriek

beneath my foot tread;

smell the broken

branch that bleeds;

taste the hollow reeds

which crackle in

a fire without flame;

while out in

the potter's field

I feel the worms

wail my name.

Serpents of another Eden.


Noli me tangere!

My body withers,

and my soul splits in two.

A death rattle

rises to my mind

thorned crown

and bloody lance

dance before my eyes.

My eyes,

they are burning

preceding me to Hell."


III


"Mea culpa, mea culpa,

mea maxima culpa.


Give me a rope!

Christ, it is dark here –

Brother, I have kissed you

to your doom.

I have fed your gentle flesh

to leeches.

God, I fear.

See my hands tremble

on the knot.


Christ, it is dark here.

Curse, Judas,

freedom is chained.

There is no rest.

My palm sweats.

The rope rots

like my maggot-full soul.


Master, your servant is damned.

My heart breaks before my neck.

The ground shakes,

Lucifer singes my beard.

A-a-a-gh the branch breaks-

damn despair - - I sink.

## "Remember"

"Amo, amas, amat, amamus,

amatis, amant"

we chanted into the dusty air –

a foreign tongue

from an alien shore.

We were asked to remember

Jupiter and his consort, Juno,

Venus, Vesta, Vulcan,

Romulus and Remus

and the nourishing wolf –

writing their names diligently

for tests that marked our path

further and further

from the core.


Today, I bend,

like a grieving willow,

to discarded roots,

to greet again

Balor of the baleful eye,

Cuchulain and Ferdia.

Finn and the Fianna,

and the magical boar

foraging the length

of Ben Bulben.

**"Karshish:**

**The Picker-up of Learning's Crumbs"**


Sometimes the Karshish in me o'ercomes the Irish.

I pick at bones unable to chew fish.

Remember the voice in the bone,

white sceptre of truth.


Sometimes the Karshish in me

stoops at the table,

I pick at crumbs of alien grain.

Remember the bone in the voice

which is broken.

Sometimes the Irish in me

o'erwhelms the Karshish,

I plunge at the heart's meat and drink the blood-red.

Remember the old kings leave only a token,

before they fall dead.


Sometimes the bread of Karshish is unfilling,

for I have drunk the bull-broth.

Remember the spell of truth, 'twas sung o'er me.

I see now the king in a dream

and cannot lie,

the Karshish is clothed, the Irish is naked.

A naked king walks before me,

as the birds throw down their cries

to sing no more.


Oh Finn, let not the water

slip through thy fingers,

but let me drink deeply.

Remember the wound that is mine.

### "Souls by the Sea"

By the holy well of the sea,

we lived in solitude,

in beehive huts –

wherein we siphoned

honey for the soul

from the pollen of our prayers.

Stones and jagged peaks –

our isolated terrain-

marked our path

to the heavenly banquet.

We relinquished the world,

like the Desert fathers before,

we fashioned on craggy peaks

and tumultuous seas

our pillars for penance

and purification.


Our dunes, the waves

our camel, the coracle.

Martyred to the flesh,

we sought the quiet

pulse of God in

the empty spaces

away, far away,

from grasping and grave men.


Our cell beds – sharp rugged rock,

our discomfort- the driven rain

veering in from the brooding vastness.

The swell of the sea,

mirrored in our heart,

and in this rhythm

the eternal murmuring of God.

# Annotations

## A Celtic Blessing

### I.  Prelude

1.  A Celtic Blessing

A blessing written in the Celtic tradition for my daughter and son-in-law on the occasion of their marriage

### II  Origins

2.  Mystery

A baby, born dying, holds on to life

3.  Enlightened

An early memory of a lamplighter

4.  Elemental

A father through the eyes of an admiring son

5.  The Pictures

The Hall and The Strand were two picture houses in Alexandria, Dunbartonshire in the 1950s

6.  Light in the Darkness

The finest gift ever

## III   History

7.  Anglesey 61 A.D.

The Romans practiced a scorched-earth policy on this sacred

island. They sought by killing the Druids to remove the head from

the Celtic tribal body.

8.  To Hell or Connaught

The cry of the bard against the loss of tradition echoes down

through the ages. Turtle Island is a Native name for North America.

9.  Las Cinco Heridas

A plea written at the height of the brutal Salvadoran civil war

(1980-1992)

10.  Las Flores de la Calle

This evokes the random killings of street urchins by the authorities in

cities in Latin America.

11. A Cleansing of the Soul

The tragedy of girls lost in the Magdalene Houses in Ireland until as late as the 1970s

**IV   The Journey**

12.  The Journey - the story

A lesson learned

13.  The Weft

Dunadd, an ancient fort in Argyllshire, where the poet was deeply moved on his first visit in 1995

14.  The Echo of the Maya

A young Guatemalan couple and a grandmother inspire by their inclusiveness and courage outside Fort Benning, Georgia, U.S.A. during a protest against The School of the Americas (WHINSEC). Julio is an everyman, representing the oppressed of Central America.

15.  Epiphany

A gift from a former student

16. The Eternal Moment

A poem inspired by the celebrated psychiatrist, who, like the poet, was born in Govanhill, Glasgow.

17. Experience

A Buddhist moment

18. The Sparrow

The transience of life

19. A Still Moment at Rattlesnake Point

A poem which came while I was reading Thomas Merton's *Confessions of a Guilty Bystander* in which he reflects on the preciousness of the moment.

20. The Coat

The epigraph is based on words spoken by an oracle in West Cork, Ireland.


**The Celtic Core**

21.. Makin'

"Makin'" is based on the Medieval term for the poets or bards of

Scotland – Makars. The poem is a meditation on the writing of poetry.

The lying in darkness and the rough stone on the flesh refer to the method used in former times by the Celtic bards in composing their poems.

22. The Beare Peninsula

A return to roots  Ferdia – man of the Goddess

23. Callanish

A chance meeting in a sacred place

24. Endurance

Reverberations of primal faiths

25. Water

Water is life.

26. Translation

A looking back to the Dinnsenchas tradition and showing the loss of meaning that can occur in translation

27. A Tremor of the Heart

A Celtic blessing for my grandchildren, Benjamin James and

Rachael Helen, on their birth in Newfoundland on March 30th, 2008.

28. The Sustainer

The second aspect of the triple – Goddess is highlighted here with echoes of Amergin (the archetypal poet of Ireland).

29. A Celtic Prayer of the Four Directions

This was inspired by a Mayan couple who read a prayer to the four directions at an anti- SOA (WHINSEC) demonstration at Fort Benning in Georgia, U.S.A. in 2005. I was impressed by the concern for the Earth in the prayer and by the inclusion of the entire world in its sentiments.

Lugh – Celtic Sun God, patron of art and craft

Brigid – Pre-Christian Irish Goddess of fire, the forge, fertility, cattle, plant-life, poetry

Dagda – He is one of the primary gods of the old Irish tradition. His name means "good God." He is good,however, not in a moral sense, but rather in that he is greatly skilled.

Cailleach – She is the third aspect of the Goddess. She represents death, change, sovereignty and transition.

Manitou - The Great Spirit

Cailleach Bheur – (Sc. Gaelic – the genteel, old lady, hag) – the
personification of winter in Scottish Gaelic folklore. She is born,
blue-faced and ugly, of the winter sun, but ends her time, as spring,
young and beautiful.

# Annotations

## Seeking the Stones

30. A Hymn for Clare Aisling

Hope and renewal brought with new life. (meine kleine Tochter –
my little daughter)

31. Brokenness

Gaps in relationships

32. The Old Man

Lamentation for an age woven into the loneliness of aging.

33. The Clyde

A cry for ecology and against spiritual poverty of today's throw-away society.

34. Dunadd

A pledge of inheritance

(cp. 13)

35. Passage Grave

An ancient monument to hope This poem is based on the tumulus at Newgrange, Co. Meath, Ireland where the light of the sun of the winter solstice penetrates the passage grave and illuminates the central chamber for fourteen minutes before moving on until the same time the following year.

36. The Chieftain

A paean of praise as the bard may have voiced it.

37. Stones

Eviction of the poor - a continuing process

38. Exile

One of the Three Sorrows of Storytelling in Ireland, the story of the Children of Lir relates how they are metamorphosed into swans by their evil stepmother, Aife. In this poem, the metamorphosis is a positive one.

"...the choice made by their lairds was real, sheep instead of men, and this was the cause of their exile and of their sorrow." John Prebble, *The Highland Clearances*

39. Felix Culpa

Judas Iscariot as an "everyman."

40. Remember

A reflection on a loss of culture which aids a little in its reclamation.

41. Karshish

The wound is the severance from the Gaelic culture- an alienation.

42. Souls by the Sea

The "green martyrdom" of the Irish monks, who following the example of the Desert fathers, sought God in isolated and rugged places.

## Biography

James J. Lafferty was born of Irish ancestry in Glasgow, Scotland in 1946 and came to Canada in 1967. His first writing began in the new land as a way to stem the pangs of the immigrant and express the heart's longings. He returned to school, in part to learn more of the poetic craft, eventually doing post-graduate studies in literature at McMaster University and, thereafter, became a high school teacher in Guelph, Ontario. He retired from his teaching post in 2009 in order to allow more time for his writing.

To date, the CD *Seeking the Stones* is Lafferty's last published work, the completion of a long-standing desire to restore the oral tradition so central to poetry since bardic times. He continues this practice in the new CD (*A Celtic Blessing*), which accompanies this book.